BASIC SKILLS AND BEYOND

SPELLING

Grades 4–5

by
Cindy Barden

illustrated by
Darcy Bell-Myers

Activities Support These Learning Outcomes

- Students will develop a range of strategies to make meaning from a variety of texts.
- Students will apply language structure and conventions, media techniques and figurative language to understand text.

Carson-Dellosa Publishing Company, Inc.
Greensboro, North Carolina

Credits:
Project Director: Sherrill B. Flora
Author: Cindy Barden
Inside illustrations: Darcy Bell-Myers
Editorial/Production: Good Neighbor Press
Cover design: Annette-Hollister-Papp

ISBN:0887241522

Table of Contents

Introduction

Activities in this book encourage students to learn spelling words as they write sentences, play games, unscramble words, complete puzzles, add suffixes and prefixes, and combine words to make compound words.

Word lists for each activity are included on parent/teacher pages. These can be used for reviews and spelling tests.

Extend the Activities

Print the spelling words for each activity on the board or chart paper before handing out the activity page.

Read the words together. Discuss the meaning of words. Ask volunteers to use the words in sentences.

Point out any homophones. Discuss the alternate spellings and meanings.

Students can design word search puzzles using spelling words. A 12 by 12 grid works well. Let students trade puzzles with a partner and solve.

Encourage students to play spelling games like Scrabble™.

Tie spelling activities in with grammar lessons. Have students identify the parts of speech of words in their spelling lists.

Give "quick quizzes." Give students three to five spelling words to write when they have a few minutes before lunch, recess, or the end of the day.

Encourage students to take home completed spelling activity pages and study the words. Ask them to write the two or three words most difficult words several times on the back of the page.

Students can write sentences, poems, letters, and stories using the words from their spelling lists.

You'll find other spelling games and activities scattered throughout this book.

Behind the Eight Ball

Page 5 can be used for reviewing spelling words for activities in this book. As you say each spelling word, ask students to write the words in the billiard balls in order.

Let students self-correct. When they finish, they can color in the billiard balls that have words spelled correctly.

Behind the Eight Ball

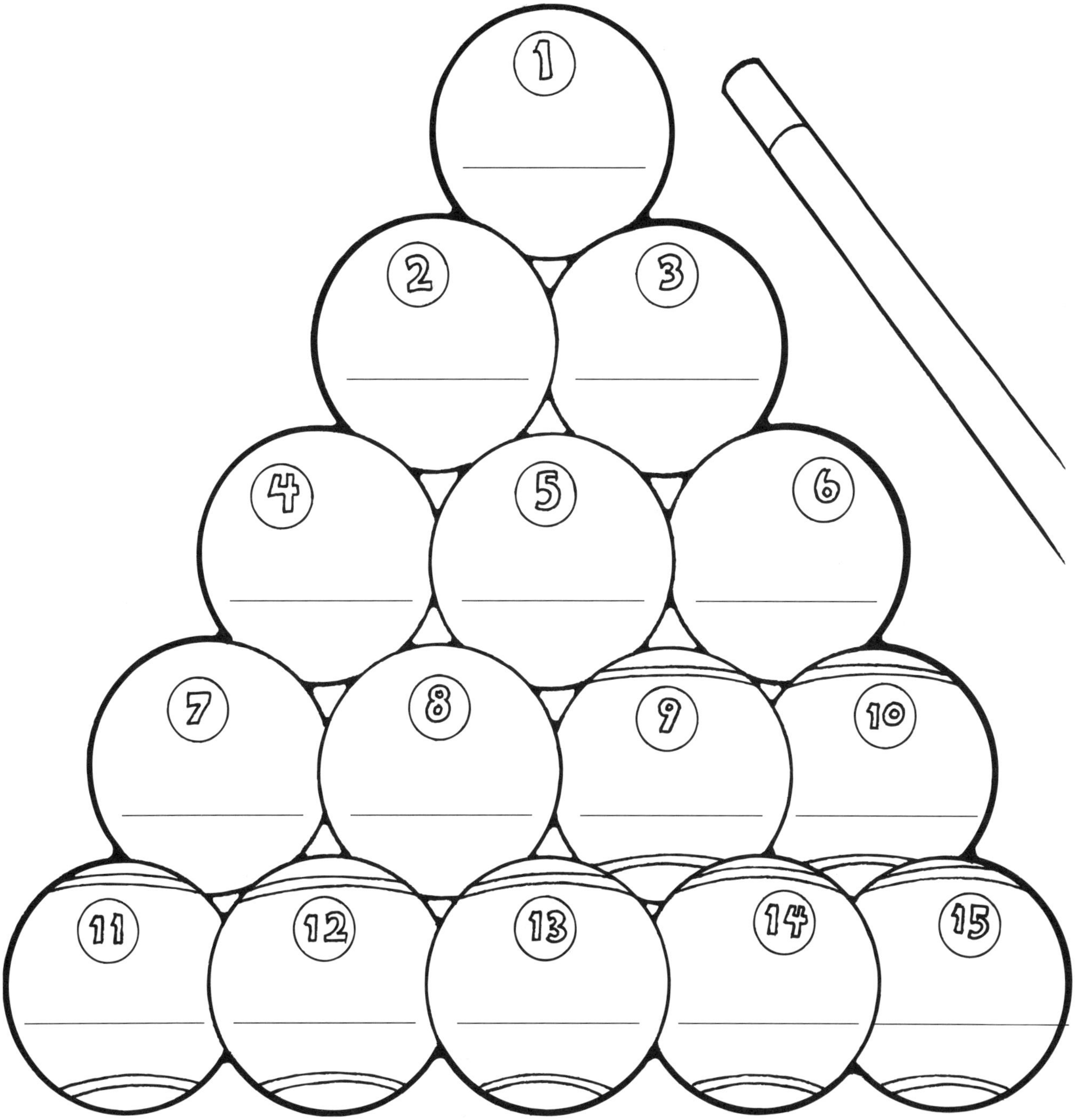

Color the billiard ball if the word is spelled correctly.

Baseball Spelling Cards

Make copies of the page of baseballs (page 7) on colored construction paper or light cardboard. Let students who have completed their other work cut apart the cards.

Write one spelling word on each card with a fine-point marker. Students with neat penmanship can help prepare cards.

You Can

. . . write the weekly spelling words on baseball cards and display in the classroom.

. . . play "Batter Up!" with the class. Directions for this baseball spelling game can be found on page 8.

Students Can

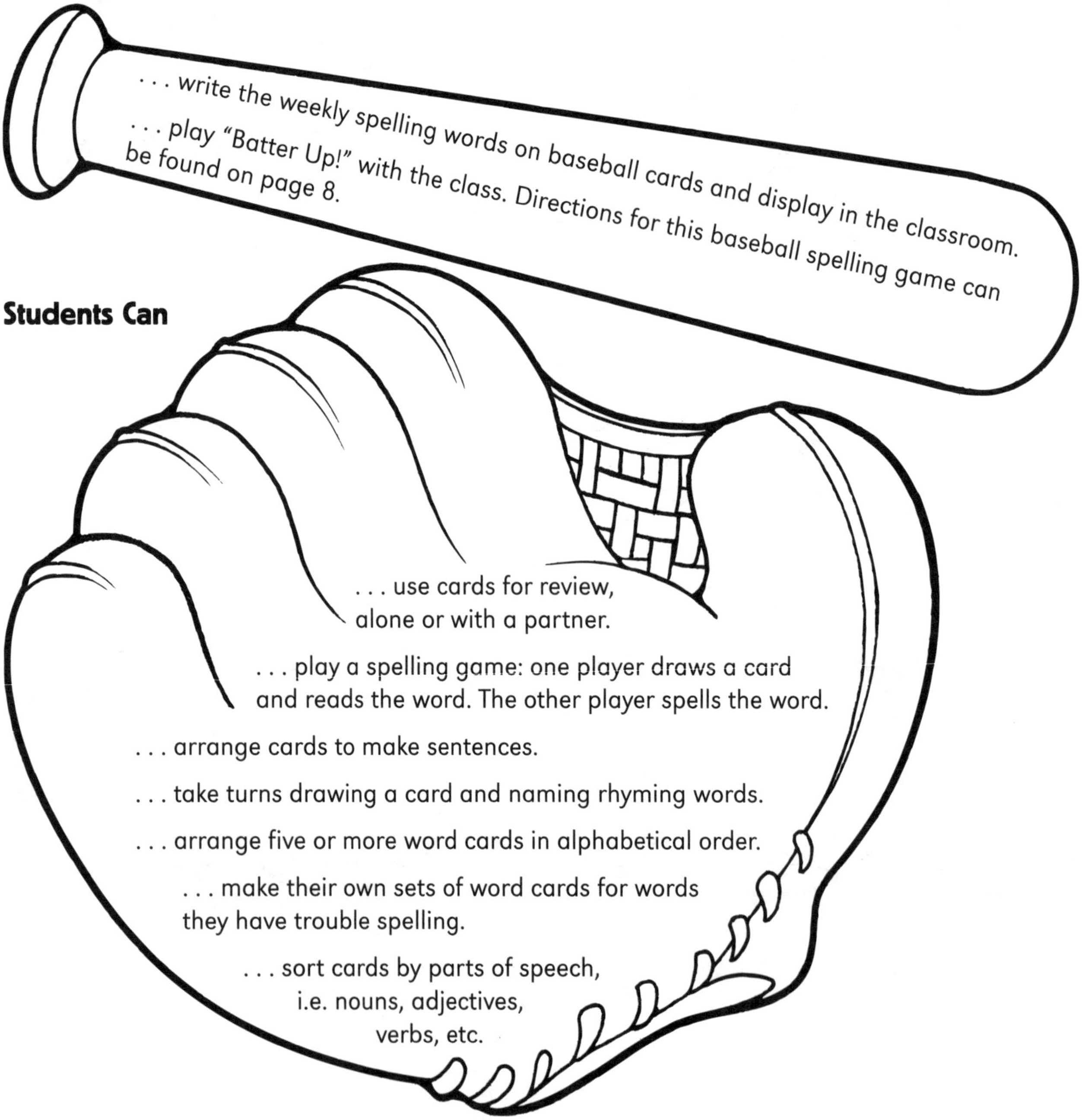

. . . use cards for review, alone or with a partner.

. . . play a spelling game: one player draws a card and reads the word. The other player spells the word.

. . . arrange cards to make sentences.

. . . take turns drawing a card and naming rhyming words.

. . . arrange five or more word cards in alphabetical order.

. . . make their own sets of word cards for words they have trouble spelling.

. . . sort cards by parts of speech, i.e. nouns, adjectives, verbs, etc.

Baseball Spelling Cards (continued)

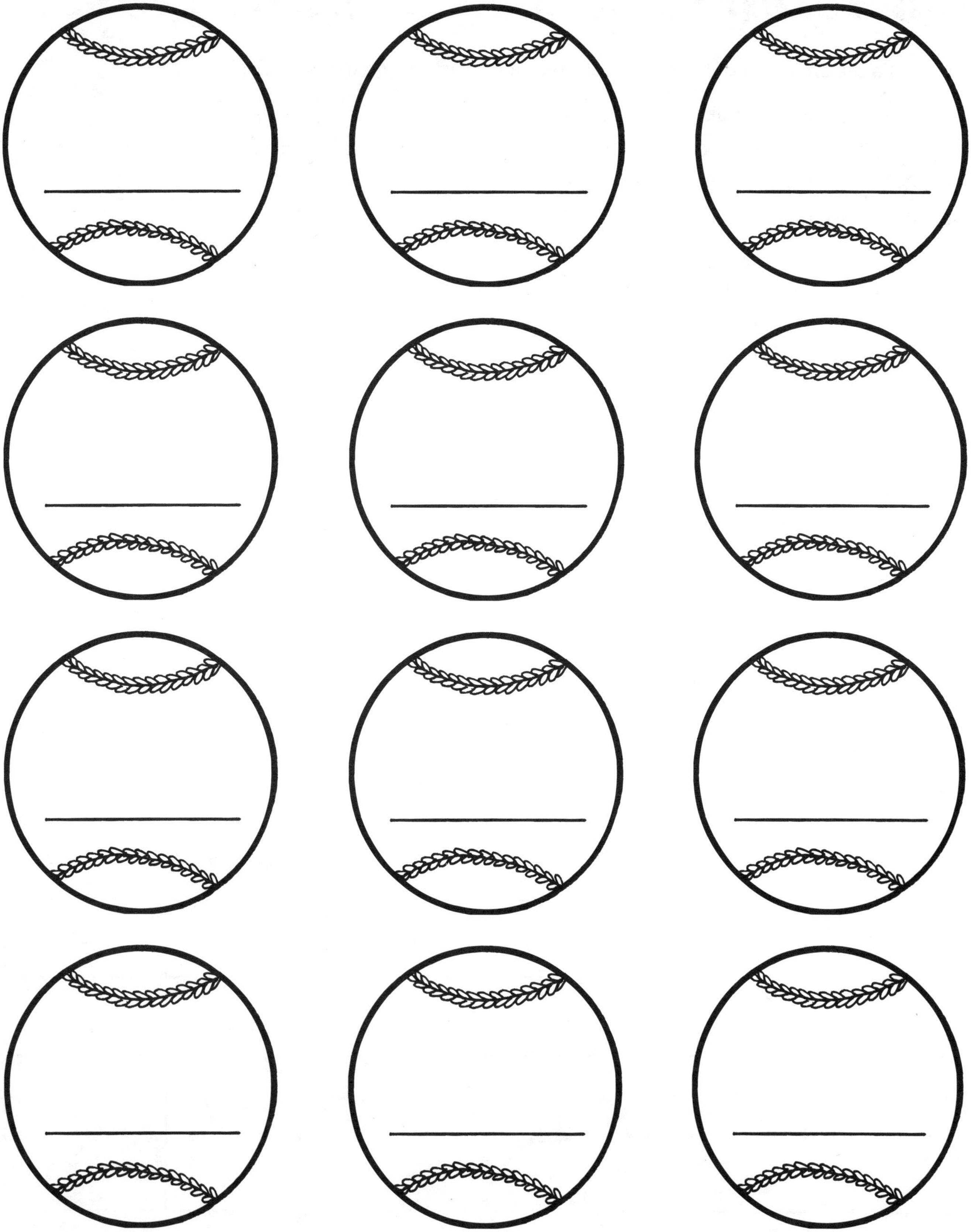

Batter Up!

You will be the umpire and the "pitcher." (Alternate, select two students to be pitchers.)

1. Place a set of baseball cards facedown in front of you.
2. Appoint one student as scorekeeper. Draw a scorecard on the board like the sample below.
3. Divide the group into two teams and select a team name.
4. Have each team line up in a separate row.
5. Draw a baseball spelling card from the top of the pile and read the word.
6. The first player in line on Team A must say the word and spell it.
7. If correct, announce, "Base hit."
   Player goes to the end of the line.
   The scorekeeper makes a tally mark in the hits column.
8. If incorrect, announce, "Sorry, you're out."
   The players goes to the end of the line.
   The scorekeeper makes a tally mark in the outs column.
   Say the word again. If the next player in line on that team can spell it correctly, the team gets a base hit.
   If not, another out.
9. Each time a player spells a word correctly, the team gets a base hit. When a team gets four base hits in the same inning, they earn a home run.
10. After a team makes three outs, the other team goes to bat.
11. Play so that both teams have the same number of "at bats."

Scorecard

Team A			Team B		
Hits	**Runs**	**Outs**	**Hits**	**Runs**	**Outs**

Word Lists for Activity Pages 10–24

Thumbs Up

calf	calm	comb
crumb	debt	doubt
gnat	half	knee
knob	know	knew
lamb	palm	thumb

A Laugh and a Half and Is Eight Enough?

bought	bright	caught
cough	dough	eight
enough	ghost	laugh
knight	neighbor	night
rough	taught	thought

Please Answer the Telephone and A Large Mammal

alphabet	autograph	biography
elephant	geography	gopher
hyphen	nephew	orphan
paragraph	pharmacy	pheasant
telephone	photograph	

You're Out! and Right on Target

blouse	cloud	clown
count	crown	flower
flour	frown	hound
hour	house	mouse
pouch	power	round
scout	sound	sour
south		

Listen to the Coach and Classes for the Coaches (plurals)

address	batch	beach
branch	brush	cause
cheese	class	coach
duplex	glass	finish
porch	radish	sandwich
search	watch	wax

Team Jerseys and Free Throw (plurals)

activity	bakery	berry
buddy	buggy	butterfly
dairy	donkey	hobby
jelly	journey	monkey
mystery	penny	puppy
valley		

Watch the Leaves Change (plurals)

calf	knife	leaf
life	thief	wife
wolf	belief	chief
hoof	proof	roof
scarf	wharf	

Note: *wharfs, scarfs,* and *hoofs* are the preferred plural. *Wharves, scarves,* and *hooves* are acceptable.

Brr . . . It's Freezing Out There and It's Not Whether You Win or Lose . . .

bought	entire	false
float	follow	forget
freeze	heavy	length
narrow	parent	repair
queen	swift	teach

Thumbs Up

Circle the letter that is silent in each word.

calf
calm
comb
crumb
debt
doubt
gnat
half
knee
knob
know
knew
lamb
palm
thumb

A Laugh and a Half

When the letters **gh** appear together in a word, they may have the sound of the letter **f**.

Examples: laugh, cough

When the letters **gh** appear together in a word, sometimes both letters are silent.

Examples: high, night, light

Write words from the spelling list.

1. **gh** sounds like **f**: ______________________________

____

____

____

2. **gh** is silent: ______________________________

____

____

____

bought
bright
caught
cough
dough
eight
enough
ghost
laugh
knight
neighbor
night
rough
taught
thought

Name ______________________________

Is Eight Enough?

Write words from the spelling list that mean the opposite.

1. cry ____________________

2. dull ____________________

3. learned ____________________

4. day ____________________

5. smooth ____________________

6. sold ____________________

Make new words. Write the new words.

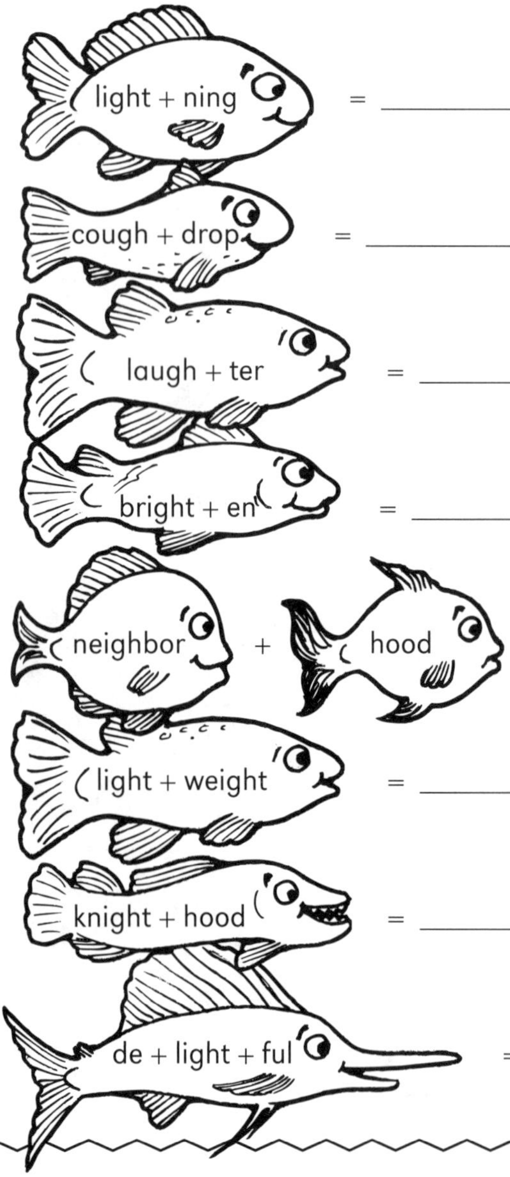

7. light + ning = ____________________

8. cough + drop = ____________________

9. laugh + ter = ____________________

10. bright + en = ____________________

11. neighbor + hood = ____________________

12. light + weight = ____________________

13. knight + hood = ____________________

14. de + light + ful = ____________________

bought
bright
caught
cough
dough
eight
enough
ghost
laugh
knight
neighbor
night
rough
taught
thought

Please Answer the Telephone

When the letters **ph** are together in a word, they usually have the sound of the letter **f**.

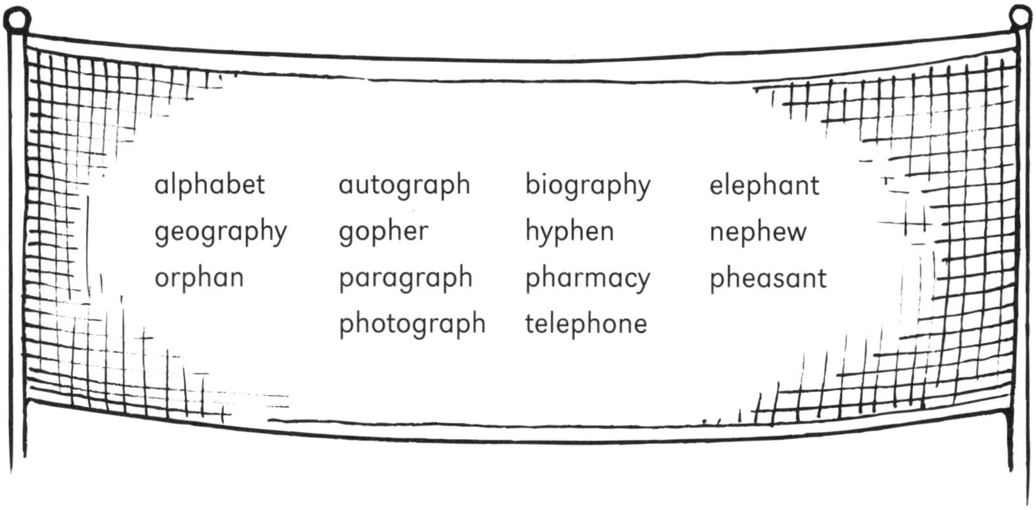

alphabet	autograph	biography	elephant
geography	gopher	hyphen	nephew
orphan	paragraph	pharmacy	pheasant
	photograph	telephone	

Write words from the spelling list to complete the sentences.

1. Joseph is my ____________________.

2. An ____________________ is a larger animal than a ____________________ or a ____________________.

3. Stephany bought cough drops at the ____________________.

4. I took many ____________________ s when I went to Memphis.

5. Ralph's favorite subject is ____________________.

6. Z is the last letter of the ____________________.

7. Our homework today is to write a ____________________ about basketball.

8. Phyllis asked the tennis champ for her ____________________.

9. The physician read a ____________________ about Marie Curie.

10. How much does it cost to make a ____________________ call to Phoenix?

A Large Mammal

Write the answers in the puzzle. Use words from the spelling list.

- alphabet
- autograph
- biography
- elephant
- geography
- gopher
- hyphen
- nephew
- orphan
- paragraph
- pharmacy
- pheasant
- telephone
- photograph

Across

1. A person's signature
3. A small mammal
4. A story about a person's life
6. A picture taken with a camera
8. A bird
11. Opposite of niece
12. A group of sentences
13. An instrument used to make calls

Down

2. A, B, C, etc.
5. Study of the land
6. Medicine store
7. A child without parents
9. A large mammal
10. Punctuation used to join words

You're Out!

When **ou** and **ow** are together in a word, they often have the same sound.

1. Write words that follow the pattern of the word at the top of each column.

clown	**found**
br ______	b ______
cr ______	gr ______
d ______	h ______
fr ______	m ______
g ______	p ______
t ______	r ______
	s ______

2. Write two words that rhyme with **blouse**.

______ ______

3. Write four words that rhyme with **flower**.

______ ______

______ ______

blouse
cloud
clown
count
crown
flower
flour
frown
hound
hour
house
mouse
pouch
power
round
scout
sound
sour
south

Name ____________________ *Diphthongs: ou and ow*

Right on Target

Look up, down, backwards, forwards, and diagonally to find the spelling words hidden in the puzzle.

				F				
			R	L	H			
			D	O	S			
		S	U	D	C	O		
		C	O	N	O	N		
	U	O	L	U	U	X	R	
	N	R	C	O	T	E	O	
D	N	U	P	H	W	H	U	D
O	W	O	N	O	O	N	N	O
W	O	L	L	U	U	U	D	W
	R	F	S	E	O	C	T	
	C	E	U	S	O	N	H	
		U	W	U	U	W		
		N	W	O	R	F		
			C	L	P			
			O	B	U			
				W				

- blouse
- cloud
- clown
- count
- crown
- flower
- flour
- frown
- hound
- house
- pouch
- power
- round
- scout
- sound
- south

Pick a Card, Any Card

Play this game with groups of four to six students.

Materials: One deck of cards for each group. The list at the bottom of the page.

To Play

1. The first player turns over the top card.
2. Leader finds the word that matches that card from the list below and says the word. Example: If the card is the two of spades, the leader says the word *doubt*.
3. Student spells the word. If correct, student keeps the card. If incorrect, student spells the word correctly for the group. Student returns the card to the bottom of the deck.
4. Play continues with students taking turns.
5. Play ends when all cards are gone. Student with the most cards wins.

	Clubs	**Spades**	**Hearts**	**Diamonds**
Ace	calf	calm	comb	crumb
2	debt	doubt	gnat	half
3	knee	knob	know	knew
4	lamb	palm	thumb	bought
5	bright	caught	cough	dough
6	eight	enough	ghost	laugh
7	knight	neighbor	night	rough
8	taught	thought	telephone	photograph
9	alphabet	autograph	biography	elephant
10	geography	gopher	hyphen	nephew
Jack	orphan	paragraph	pharmacy	pheasant
Queen	blouse	cloud	clown	count
King	crown	flower	flour	sound

Name ______________________________

Listen to the Coach

Add **s** to most words to make them plural.

Example: book + s = books

Add **es** to words that end in **sh**, **ch**, **s**, **x**, or **z.**

Examples: wish + es = wishes
tax + es = taxes

Write the **plurals** of each word in the spelling list.

1. ______________
2. ______________
3. ______________
4. ______________
5. ______________
6. ______________
7. ______________
8. ______________
9. ______________
10. ______________
11. ______________
12. ______________
13. ______________
14. ______________
15. ______________
16. ______________
17. ______________
18. ______________

address
batch
beach
branch
brush
cause
cheese
class
coach
duplex
glass
finish
porch
radish
sandwich
search
watch
wax

Classes for the Coaches

address
batch
beach
branch
brush
cause
cheese
class
coach
duplex
glass
finish
porch
radish
sandwich
search
watch
wax

Write the **plural** forms of the words from the spelling list that match the clues.

Use a dictionary if you are not sure of the meaning of a word.

1. Two-family homes: ____________________

2. Peanut butter and jelly: ____________________

3. They help you see better: ____________________

4. Reasons why things happen: ____________________

5. What we have in school: ____________________

6. Parts of a tree: ____________________

7. Garden vegetables: ____________________

8. Places to sit in the summer: ____________________

9. What people use to tell time: ____________________

10. Sandy places: ____________________

11. Endings: ____________________

12. Dairy products: ____________________

Team Jerseys

If a word ends in a consonant followed by **y**, change the y to **i** and add **es** to make it **plural**.

Examples: cherry – y + i + es = cherries
jersey + s = jerseys

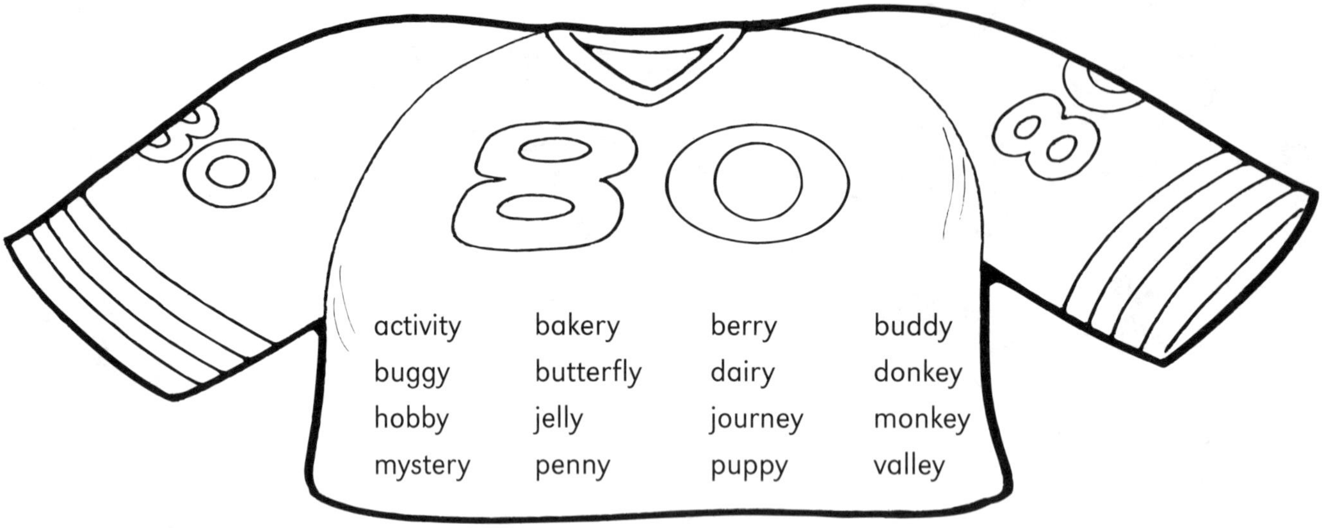

Write the **plurals** for the words from the spelling list.

1. ____________ **9.** ____________

2. ____________ **10.** ____________

3. ____________ **11.** ____________

4. ____________ **12.** ____________

5. ____________ **13.** ____________

6. ____________ **14.** ____________

7. ____________ **15.** ____________

8. ____________ **16.** ____________

Write the **plural** of four other words that end in **y**.

17. ____________ **19.** ____________

18. ____________ **20.** ____________

Free Throw

Color the jerseys if both words are spelled correctly.

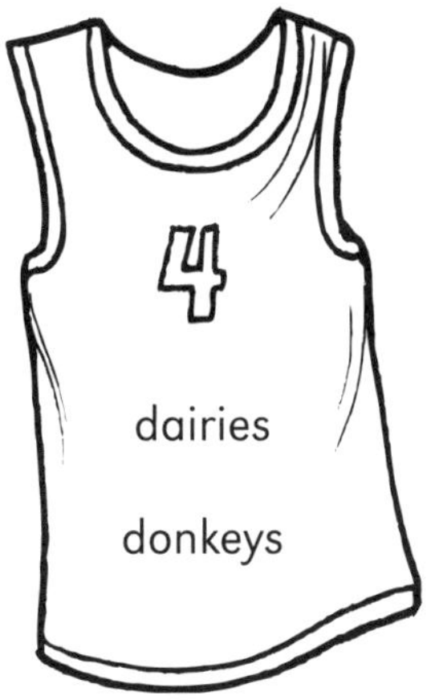

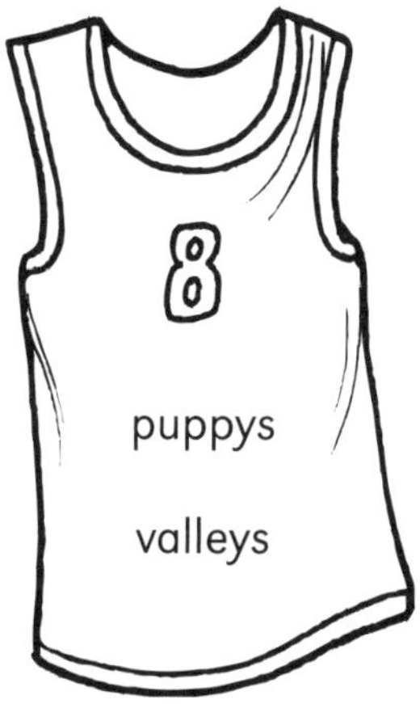

Watch the Leaves Change

These words form the **plural** by changing the **f** or **fe** to **v** and adding **es**.

Example: calf − f + v + es = calves

Write the **plural** of these words.

1. knife ____________________
2. leaf ____________________
3. life ____________________
4. thief ____________________
5. wife ____________________
6. wolf ____________________

These words form the **plural** by adding **s**.

Example: belief + s = beliefs

belief	chief	hoof	proof
roof	scarf	wharf	

Write the **plural** of the words in the sentences.

7. A horse has four ____________________.
8. All the cars' ____________________ were dented from the hail.
9. Tina wore three ____________________ to keep warm.
10. Keegan's ____________________ about money are very strong.

calf
knife
leaf
life
thief
wife
wolf
belief
chief
hoof
proof
roof
scarf
wharf

Brrr . . . It's Freezing Out There

bought
entire
false
float
follow
forget
freeze
heavy
length
narrow
parent
repair
queen
swift
teach

Write sentences that use the spelling words listed. Underline the spelling words in your sentences.

1. queen; parent ____________________

____

2. float; swift ____________________

____

3. parent; repair ____________________

____

4. bought; entire ____________________

____

5. false; follow ____________________

____

6. freeze; forget ____________________

____

7. narrow; length; heavy ____________________

____

It's Not Whether You Win or Lose . . .

Write words from the spelling list that are the opposites.

1.	break	________	**9.**	sink	________
2.	child	________	**10.**	sold	________
3.	king	________	**11.**	slow	________
4.	lead	________	**12.**	thaw	________
5.	learn	________	**13.**	true	________
6.	light	________	**14.**	wide	________
7.	part	________	**15.**	width	________
8.	remember	________			

bought
entire
false
float
follow
forget
freeze
heavy
length
narrow
parent
repair
queen
swift
teach

Word Lists for Activity Pages 26–37

Race to the Finish and Strikes Are Great . . .

depart	equal
glance	faithful
feast	hidden
impossible	invite
lonely	lovely
manage	prepare
refuse	remember
speed	spoil
welcome	wisdom

Pregame Warm-Ups

nonfat	nonsense
nonskid	preschool
preview	uncertain
uncommon	unhappy
unpaid	

It's Not Impossible

below	beware
imperfect	impolite
improper	incomplete
incorrect	indirect
misplace	misspell

Instant Replay

decode	defrost
derail	disappear
dislike	disobey
rebuild	repaint
research	subfloor
submarine	subway

All Through the Year and Mixed up Months and Days

Sunday	Monday
Tuesday	Wednesday
Thursday	Friday
Saturday	January
February	March
April	May
June	July
August	September
October	November
December	

To Double or Not to Double

darkness	dangerous
bigger	largest
cooked	flowery
avoidance	paintable
writing	creativity
cheerful	quickly

Note: Like most spelling rules for the English language, there are exceptions to this rule. Words ending in **-ow** do not double the final consonant when adding in **-ing**. The **-ow** combination works more like two vowels at the end of a word.

Change the Y to I

bumpier	bumpiest
busier	busiest
dustier	dustiest
earlier	earliest
emptiness	grayer
grayest	happiness
playing	prettier
prettiest	silliness
sleepiness	sleepily
studying	

Name ______________________________ *Word search puzzle*

Race to the Finish

Circle the words from the spelling list. Look up, down, forward, backward, and diagonally.

N	O	W	I	S	T	H	R	C	S	R
I	N	V	I	T	E	S	U	F	E	R
R	N	I	B	Y	R	C	D	B	T	E
M	E	E	L	F	S	A	M	G	G	F
H	P	E	D	P	R	E	P	A	R	E
L	V	O	E	D	M	W	N	E	C	A
O	I	E	S	E	I	A	J	N	D	S
N	D	K	R	S	M	H	A	L	P	T
E	N	O	D	P	I	L	Q	O	R	R
L	T	O	U	V	G	B	I	W	Y	Z
Y	M	E	Q	U	A	L	L	B	C	C
R	E	N	E	M	O	C	L	E	W	Q

depart
equal
faithful
feast
glance
hidden
impossible
invite
lonely
lovely
manage
prepare
refuse
remember
speed
spoil
welcome
wisdom

Strikes Are Great—If You're Bowling

Write a word that means the same or nearly the same as the word in the spelling list. Use a dictionary or thesaurus if you need help.

1. depart	______________	**2.** equal	______________
3. glance	______________	**4.** faithful	______________
5. feast	______________	**6.** hidden	______________
7. impossible	______________	**8.** invite	______________
9. lonely	______________	**10.** lovely	______________
11. manage	______________	**12.** prepare	______________
13. refuse	______________	**14.** remember	______________
15. speed	______________	**16.** spoil	______________
17. welcome	______________	**18.** wisdom	______________

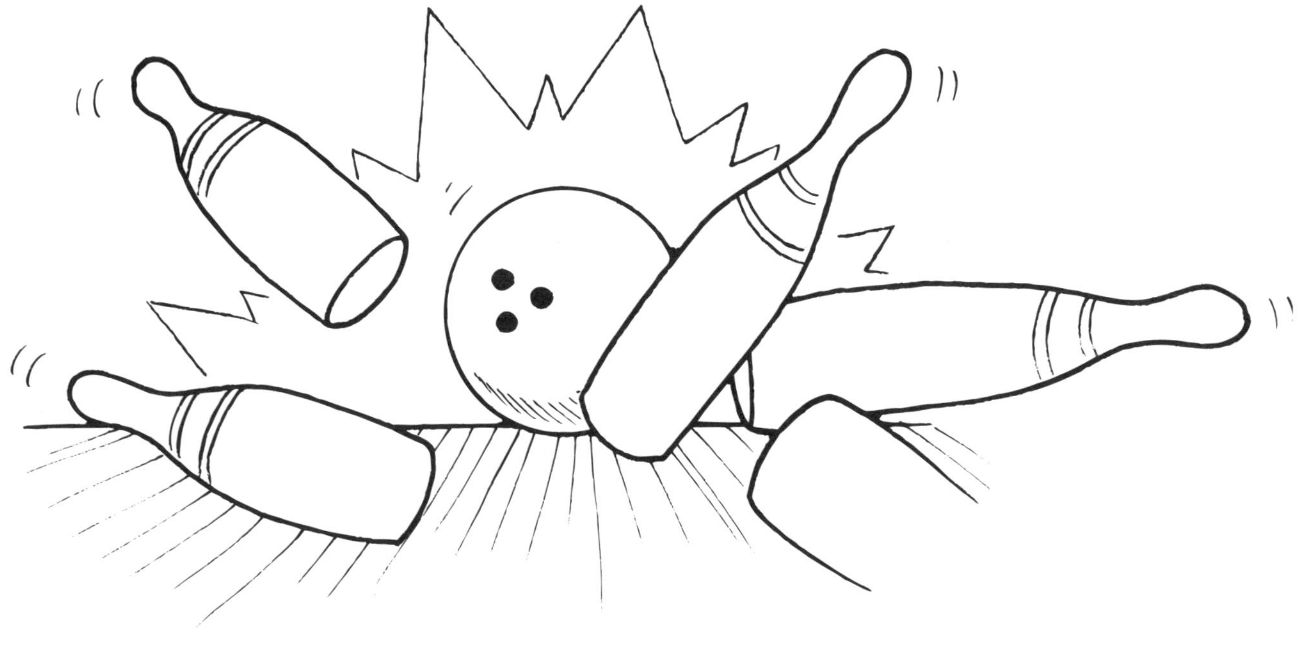

Name ______________________________

Pregame Warm-Ups

A prefix is a group of letters added at the beginning of a base word. A prefix changes the meaning of a word.

Prefix		**Base word**		**New word**
un	+	safe	=	unsafe
pre	+	game	=	pregame
non	+	stop	=	nonstop

Add the prefix **-un**, **-non**, or **-pre** to the base words.

Write the new words with a short definition.

1. view: ______________________________
2. happy: ______________________________
3. paid: ______________________________
4. fat: ______________________________
5. certain: ______________________________
6. common: ______________________________
7. sense: ______________________________
8. school: ______________________________
9. skid: ______________________________
10. What does the prefix **-un** mean? ______________________________
11. What does the prefix **-pre** mean? ______________________________
12. What does the prefix **-non** mean? ______________________________

Name ______________________________ *Prefixes: in-, be-, mis-, im-*

It's Not Impossible

Add the prefix **in-** or **be-** to the base words.

Write the new words.

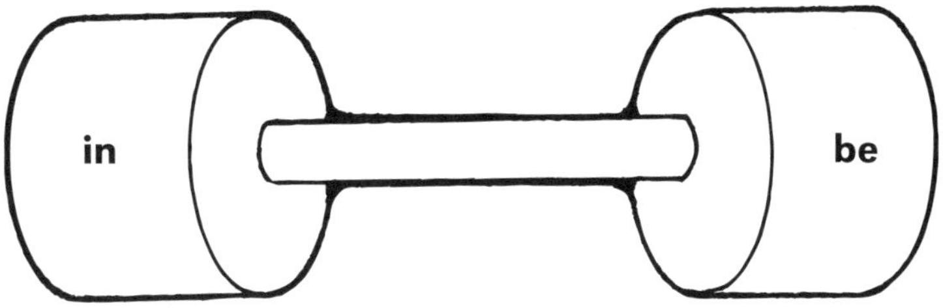

1.	________	+	correct	=	____________________
2.	________	+	low	=	____________________
3.	________	+	complete	=	____________________
4.	________	+	ware	=	____________________
5.	________	+	direct	=	____________________

Add the prefix **mis-** or **im-** to the base word.

Write the new words.

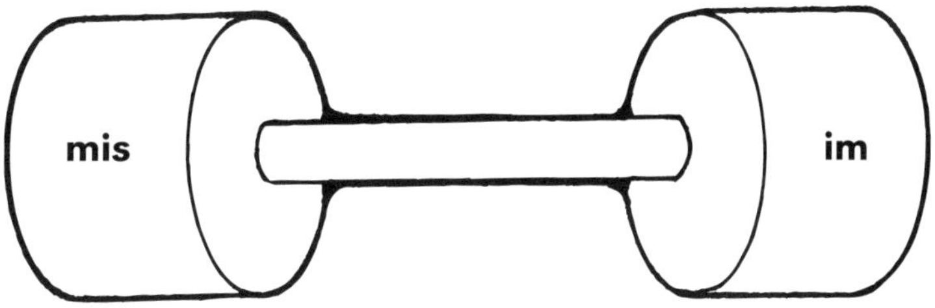

6.	________	+	proper	=	____________________
7.	________	+	polite	=	____________________
8.	________	+	place	=	____________________
9.	________	+	perfect	=	____________________
10.	________	+	spell	=	____________________

Name ______________________________ *Prefixes: re-, dis-, sub-, de-*

Instant Replay

Add **re-**, **dis-**, **sub-**, or **de-** to the base words. Write the new words.

1. ________ + search = ____________________
2. ________ + rail = ____________________
3. ________ + appear = ____________________
4. ________ + floor = ____________________
5. ________ + code = ____________________
6. ________ + way = ____________________
7. ________ + obey = ____________________
8. ________ + frost = ____________________
9. ________ + build = ____________________
10. ________ + like = ____________________
11. ________ + marine = ____________________
12. ________ + paint = ____________________

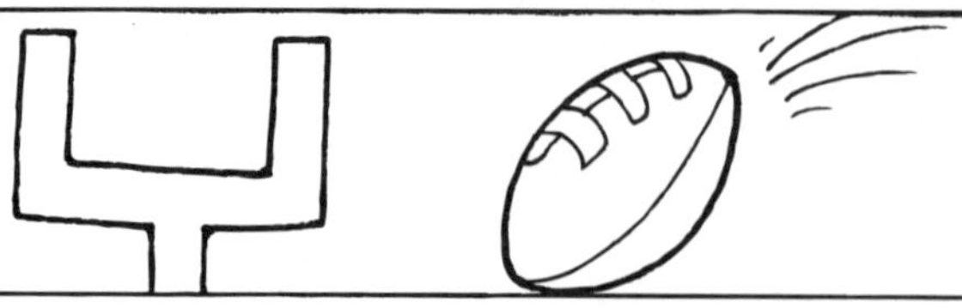

Name ______________________________

It's All Downhill

Circle the prefixes. Underline the base words.

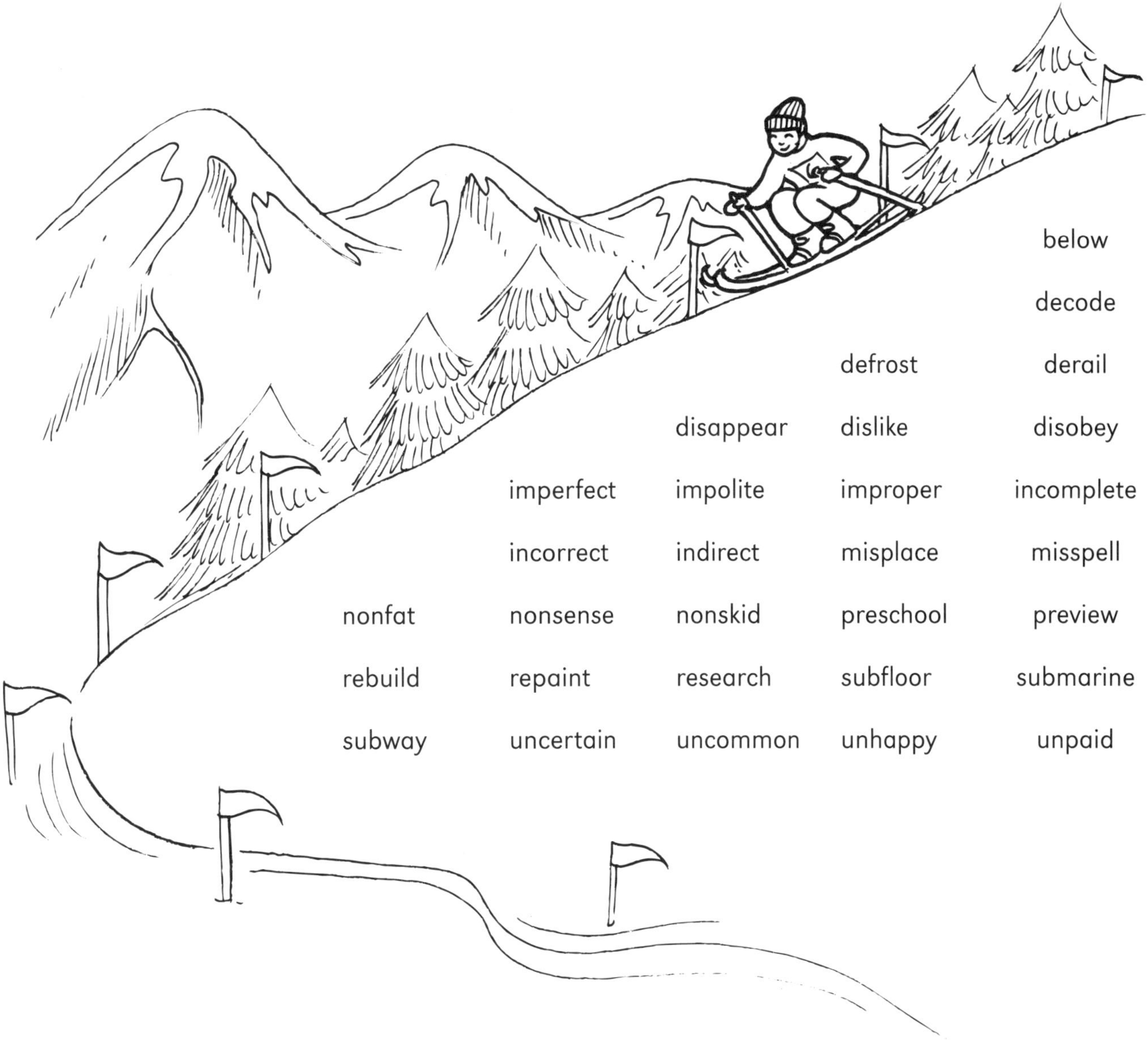

below
decode
defrost derail
disappear dislike disobey
imperfect impolite improper incomplete
incorrect indirect misplace misspell
nonfat nonsense nonskid preschool preview
rebuild repaint research subfloor submarine
subway uncertain uncommon unhappy unpaid

Name ______________________________________

All Through the Year

The names of the days of the week and months of the year always begin with a capital letter.

1. What day is today? ____________________

2. What month is it? ____________________

3. What month were you born? ____________________

4. What is you favorite month? ____________________

5. Write the names of the first six months of the year in alphabetical order. (January through June).

____

____

____

____

____

____

Circle the words that are spelled correctly.

6. Wednesday
wednesday

7. Thursday
Thirsday

8. Apirl
April

9. Twosdsay
Tuesday

10. saturday
Saturday

11. Feburary
February

Sunday
Monday
Tuesday
Wednesday
Thursday
Friday
Saturday
January
February
March
April
May
June
July
August
September
October
November
December

Name ______________________________

Mixed-Up Months and Days

Unscramble the letters. Write the words. Don't forget to capitalize the first letter of each word.

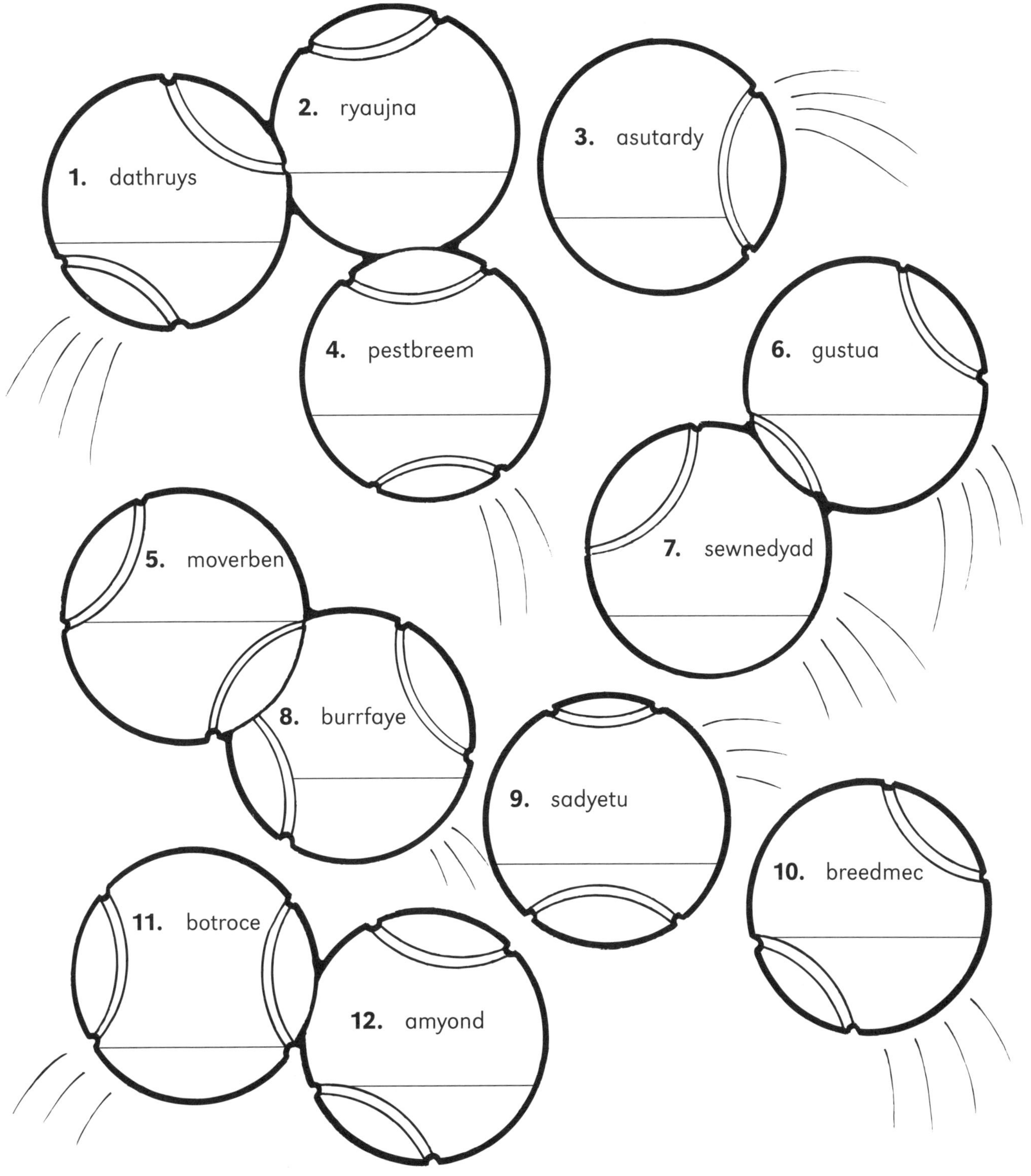

Climbing Mount Everest

Always capitalize the first word and all important words in the names of cities, states, and countries.

Example: United States of America

1. Write the name of the city where you live. ______________________

2. Write the name of the state where you live. ______________________

3. Write the name of two countries. ______________________

____

Always capitalize the names of islands, bodies of water, mountains, and volcanoes.

Examples: Mount Saint Helens
Atlantic Ocean

4. Write the name of a mountain. ______________________

5. Write the name of a body of water. ______________________

Circle the words that should be capitalized.

6. When we went to honolulu, hawaii, we went swimming in the pacific ocean.

7. Did you ever take a boat ride on the mississippi river?

8. paris is the capital of france.

9. The city of denver is in the rocky mountains.

10. mount fuji is a volcano on honshu island in japan.

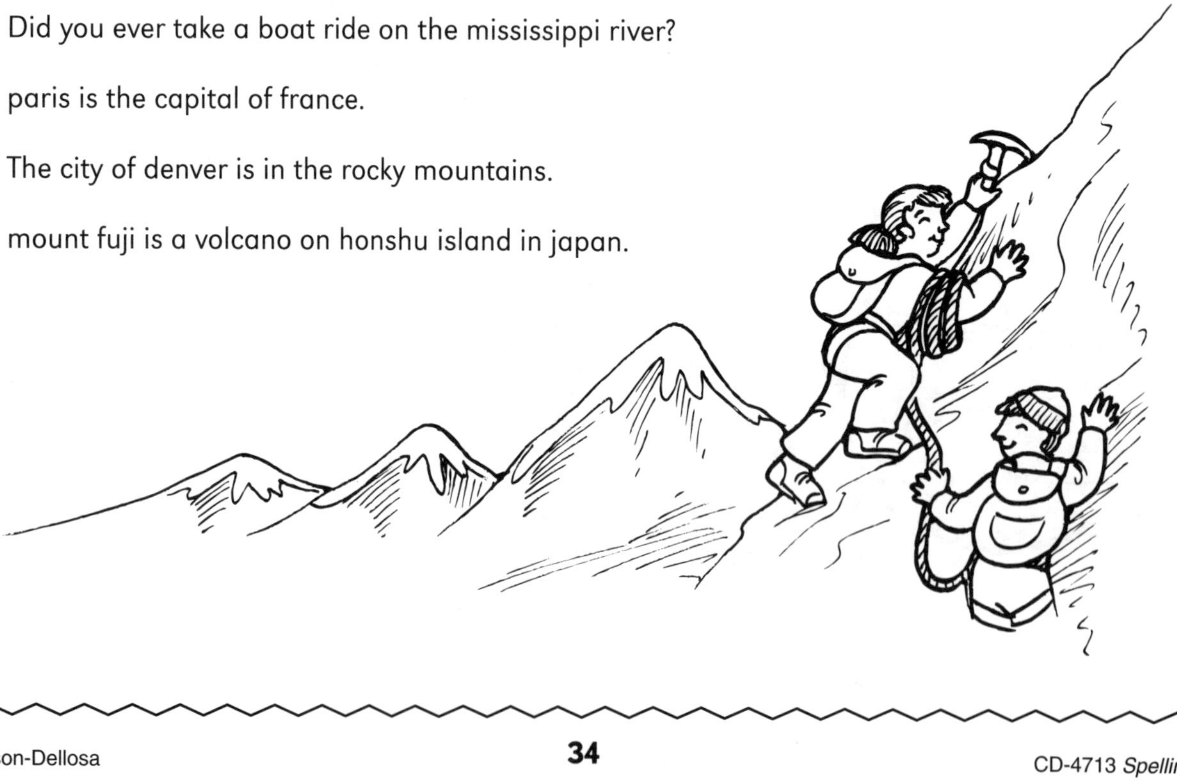

Name ______________________

To Double or Not to Double

When a one–syllable word ends in one vowel and one consonant, double the final consonant before adding a suffix that begins with a vowel.

Base word		Suffix		New word
slip + p	+	ing	=	slipping
slip + p	+	ery	=	slippery

When a word ends in **e**, drop the final **e** before adding a suffix that begins with a vowel.

Examples:			
	peace - e + able	=	peaceable
	large - e + er	=	larger

Do not drop the final **e** when adding a suffix that begins with a consonant.

Examples:			
	peace + ful	=	peaceful
	blame + less	=	blameless

Add the suffixes. Write the new words.

1. dark + ness = ______________

2. danger + ous = ______________

3. big + er = ______________

4. large + est = ______________

5. cook + ed = ______________

6. flower + ery = ______________

7. avoid + ance = ______________

8. paint + able = ______________

9. write + ing = ______________

10. create + ity = ______________

11. cheer + ful = ______________

12. quick + ly = ______________

Name ______________________________

Tic, Tac, Double

If the last consonant should be doubled before adding a suffix beginning with a vowel, draw an X over the word. If the last consonant should not be doubled before adding a suffix beginning with a vowel, draw an O over the word.

1.

sit	chop	cheer
call	ask	drip
lock	shop	quick

2.

grin	slip	hunt
paint	trick	grant
fall	cook	big

3.

drop	feed	trick
jog	rock	hug
run	pet	bump

4.

hum	park	blink
rain	plan	trap
get	join	swim

5.

help	win	dip
quick	bag	plant
step	cup	shout

Name ______________________________

Change the Y to I

When a word ends in a vowel and a **y**, do not change the **y** before adding the suffix.

Base word		**Suffix**		**New word**
annoy	+	ed	=	annoyed
buy	+	er	=	buyer

When a word ends in a consonant and a **y**, change the **y** to **i** before adding a suffix.

busy	-	y	+	i	+	er	=	busier
beauty	-	y	+	i	+	ful	=	beautiful

Exception: When adding **-ing**, do not change the **y** to **i**.

carry	+	ing	=	carrying

Add suffixes. Write the new words.

	+ er	**+ est**
1. bumpy	______________	______________
2. busy	______________	______________
3. dusty	______________	______________
4. early	______________	______________
5. gray	______________	______________
6. pretty	______________	______________

	+ ness	**+ ly**
7. silly	______________	______________
8. empty	______________	______________
9. happy	______________	______________
10. sleepy	______________	______________

	+ ing
11. play	______________
12. study	______________

Word Lists for Activity Pages 39–43

Simply Marvelous!

dangerous, breathless, treatable, hopeful, hopeless, wonderful
friendly, friendless, careful, careless, bravely

Dive In

bravely, comfortable, emptiness, friendly, happiness, having
jogged, peaceful, sillier, smiling, spelling, swimming
thinnest, useless

Circle the Words and Score a Goal

ceiling, computer, curtain, garage, listen, mountain
pencil, pillow, tongue, scissors, wheel, whisper

Play according to directions on page 17.

	Clubs	Spades	Hearts	Diamonds
Ace	frown	hound	house	pouch
2	power	round	scout	south
3	address	batch	beach	branch
4	brush	cause	cheese	class
5	coach	duplex	glass	finish
6	porch	radish	sandwich	search
7	watch	wax	scarf	wharf
8	activity	bakery	berry	buddy
9	buggy	butterfly	dairy	donkey
10	hobby	jelly	journey	monkey
Jack	mystery	penny	puppy	valley
Queen	calf	knife	leaf	life
King	thief	wife	wolf	belief

	Clubs	Spades	Hearts	Diamonds
Ace	chief	hoof	proof	roof
2	bought	entire	false	float
3	follow	forget	freeze	heavy
4	length	narrow	parent	repair
5	queen	swift	teach	scissors
6	dangerous	breathless	treatable	hopeful
7	hopeless	wonderful	friendly	tongue
8	friendless	careful	careless	bravely
9	bravely	comfortable	emptiness	friendly
10	happiness	having	jogged	peaceful
Jack	sillier	smiling	spelling	swimming
Queen	thinnest	useless	wheel	whisper
King	ceiling	computer	curtain	garage

Name ____

Simply Marvelous!

A suffix is a group of letters added to the end of a base word. A suffix changes the meaning of a word.

Base word		**Suffix**		**New word**
marvel	+	ous	=	marvelous
time	+	less	=	timeless
bend	+	able	=	bendable

Add a suffix to each word. Use **-ous**, **-less**, **-ly**, **-able**, or **-ful**.

Write a short definition for each new word.

1. danger + __________ = ________________

____

2. breath + __________ = ________________

____

3. treat + __________ = ________________

____

4. hope + __________ = ________________

____

5. wonder + __________ = ________________

____

6. friend + __________ = ________________

____

7. care + __________ = ________________

____

8. brave + __________ = ________________

____

Dive In

Divide each word into its base word and its suffix.

	Base word	Suffix
1. happiness	____________	________
2. useless	____________	________
3. thinnest	____________	________
4. spelling	____________	________
5. bravely	____________	________
6. sillier	____________	________
7. friendly	____________	________
8. emptiness	____________	________
9. smiling	____________	________
10. having	____________	________
11. comfortable	____________	________
12. jogged	____________	________
13. swimming	____________	________
14. peaceful	____________	________

Name ______________________________

Before or After?

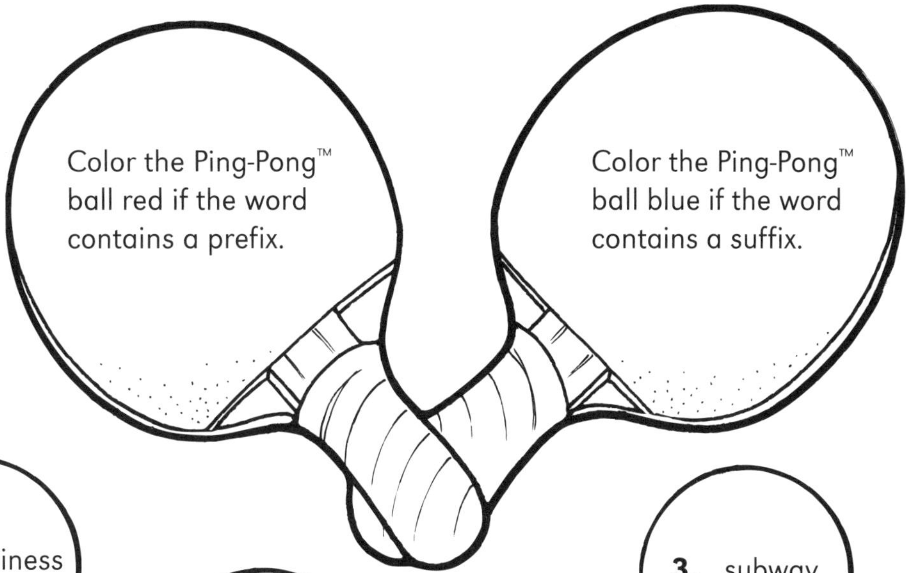

1. happiness
2. research
3. subway
4. swimming
5. preschool
6. breathless
7. careful
8. unhappy
9. rewrite
10. bumpier
11. playing
12. largest
13. incorrect
14. creativity

Name ______________________________

Circle the Words

Look up, down, forwards, and backwards to find the words from the spelling list in the puzzle.

- ceiling
- computer
- curtain
- garage
- listen
- mountain
- pencil
- pillow
- tongue
- scissors
- wheel
- whisper

C	O	M	P	U	T	E	R	O	O	S	T
E	L	A	E	W	H	I	S	P	E	R	H
I	I	R	N	H	L	N	O	T	T	O	C
L	V	C	C	E	I	I	E	Y	N	S	U
I	E	H	I	E	S	A	U	T	E	S	G
N	P	U	L	L	T	T	G	S	S	I	H
G	A	R	A	G	E	R	N	I	E	C	E
R	N	I	A	T	N	U	O	M	P	S	I
O	E	Y	D	N	A	C	T	A	P	T	I
U	V	A	L	U	E	L	A	R	O	C	V
P	I	L	L	O	W	O	R	S	T	A	D
S	G	L	O	V	E	M	Y	H	R	F	A

Look for other words in the puzzle not listed above. Circle them with a red pen or pencil and write them below.

Four-letter words found: ______________________________

____

Five-letter words found: ______________________________

____

Six-letter words found: ______________________________

____

Score a Goal

An analogy compares two things that go together in the same way.

Examples: Stick is to hockey as bat is to baseball.
A window is to glass as a chair is to wood.

ceiling
computer
curtain
garage
listen
mountain
pencil
pillow
tongue
scissors
wheel
whisper

Write words from the spelling list to complete the analogies.

1. Floor is to below as ____________ is to above.
2. ____________ is to soft as wood is to hard.
3. ____________ is to steering as brakes are to stopping.
4. Clothes are to closet as car is to ____________.
5. Rug is to floor as ____________ is to window.
6. Keyboard is to ____________ as wheel is to car.
7. ____________ is to high as valley is to low.
8. ____________ is to taste as nose is to smell.
9. ____________ are to paper as saw is to wood.
10. Watch is to TV as ____________ is to radio.

Finish these analogies.

11. Whisper is to ____________ as ____________ is to ____________.
12. Pencil is to ____________ as ____________ is to ____________.

Test Time

One or more silent letters are missing in each word. Rewrite the words correctly.

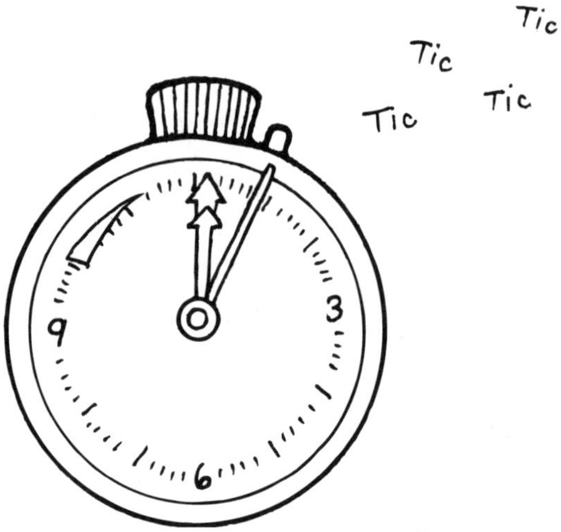

1. neibor ____________
2. thout ____________
3. thum ____________
4. gost ____________
5. caf ____________
6. dout ____________

Circle the word in each pair that is spelled correctly.

7.	coachs	coaches	**11.**	blouse	blowse
8.	waxes	waxs	**12.**	scout	scowt
9.	branches	branchess	**13.**	flouer	flower
10.	clowd	cloud	**14.**	porches	porchs

Write the plural for each word.

15. butterfly ____________
16. monkey ____________
17. activity ____________
18. valley ____________
19. penny ____________
20. puppy ____________
21. wife ____________
22. leaf ____________

Name ______________________________

Test Time (2)

Combine two words with the prefix listed in each row. Write the new words.

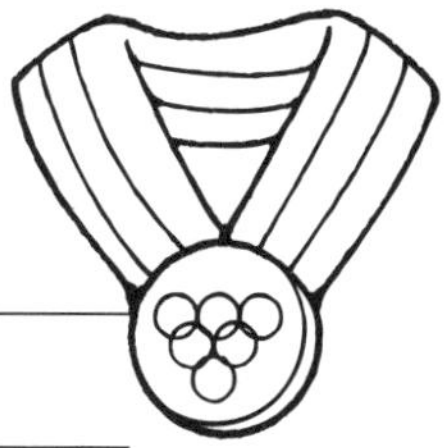

Example: un—unhappy unsafe

1. pre ______________ ______________
2. non ______________ ______________
3. in ______________ ______________
4. be ______________ ______________
5. mis ______________ ______________
6. im ______________ ______________
7. re ______________ ______________
8. dis ______________ ______________
9. sub ______________ ______________
10. de ______________ ______________

Combine two words with the suffix listed in each row. Write the new words.

11. ing ______________ ______________
12. er ______________ ______________
13. est ______________ ______________
14. ful ______________ ______________
15. ly ______________ ______________
16. ness ______________ ______________
17. ous ______________ ______________
18. less ______________ ______________
19. able ______________ ______________
20. Write three compound words: ______________

______________ ______________

Answer Key

Thumbs Up 10

1. l	2. b	3. g
4. l	5. b	6. l
7. b	8. k	9. k
10. l	11. b	12. b
13. k	14. k	15. b

A Laugh and a Half 11

1. cough; enough; laugh; rough
2. bought; bright; caught; dough; eight; ghost; knight neighbor; night; taught; thought

Is Eight Enough? 12

1. laugh
2. bright
3. taught
4. night
5. rough
6. bought
7. lightning
8. cough drop
9. laughter
10. brighten
11. neighborhood
12. lightweight
13. knighthood
14. delightful

Please Answer the Telephone 13

1. nephew
2. elephant; gopher; pheasant
3. pharmacy
4. photograph
5. geography
6. alphabet
7. paragraph
8. autograph
9. biography
10. telephone

A Large Mammal 14

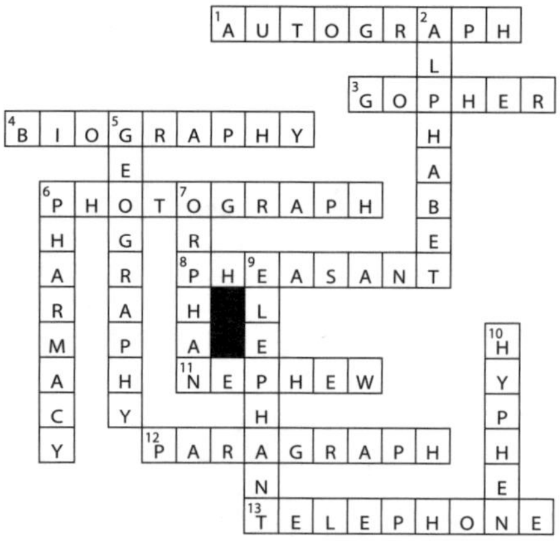

You're Out! 15

2. mouse and house
3. hour, power, sour, (flour), tower

Right on Target 16

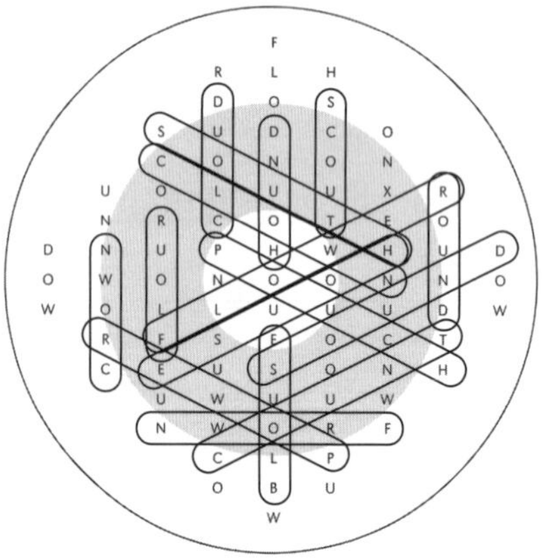

Listen to the Coach 18

Word order may vary: addresses; batches; beaches; branches; brushes; causes; cheeses; classes; coaches; duplexes; glasses; finishes; porches; radishes; sandwiches; searches; watches; waxes

Classes for the Coaches ... 19

1. duplexes	2. sandwiches
3. glasses	4. causes
5. classes	6. branches
7. radishes	8. porches
9. watches	10. beaches
11. finishes	12. cheeses

Team Jerseys 20

Word order may vary: activities; bakeries; berries; buddies; buggies; butterflies; dairies; donkeys; hobbies; jellies; journeys; monkeys; mysteries; pennies; puppies; valleys

Free Throw 21

All jerseys should be colored except 3, 5, and 8.

Watch the Leaves Change 22

1. knives
2. leaves
3. lives
4. thieves
5. wives
6. wolves
7. hoofs (hooves)
8. roofs
9. scarfs (scarves)
10. beliefs

It's Not Whether You Win or Lose 24

1. repair	2. parent
3. queen	4. follow
5. teach	6. heavy
7. entire	8. forget
9. float	10. bought
11. swift	12. freeze
13. false	14. narrow
15. length	

Answer Key

Race to the Finish 26

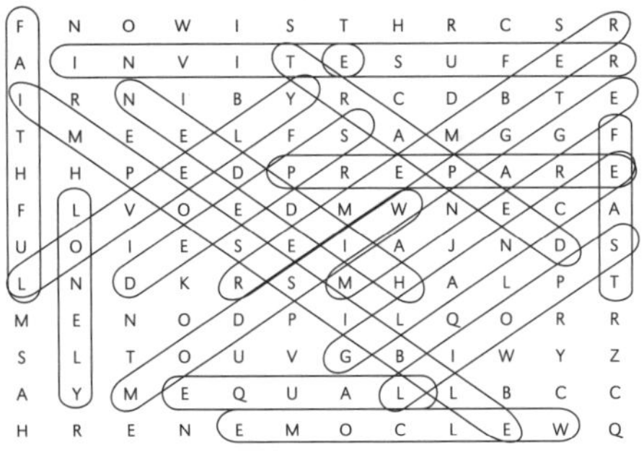

Pregame Warm-Ups 28

1. preview 2. unhappy
3. prepaid 4. nonfat
5. uncertain 6. uncommon
7. nonsense 8. preschool
9. nonskid 10. not
11. before 12. not

It's Not Impossible 29

1. incorrect 2. below
3. incomplete 4. beware
5. indirect 6. improper
7. impolite 8. misplace
9. imperfect 10. misspell

Instant Replay 30

1. research 2. derail
3. disappear 4. subfloor
5. decode 6. subway
7. disobey 8. defrost
9. rebuild 10. dislike
11. submarine 12. repaint

All Through the Year 32

5. April/February/January/June/March/May
6. Wednesday
7. Thursday
8. April
9. Tuesday
10. Saturday
11. February

Mixed-Up Months and Days 33

1. Thursday 2. January
3. Saturday 4. September
5. November 6. August
7. Wednesday 8. February
9. Tuesday 10. December
11. October 12. Monday

Climbing Mount Everest... 34

6. Honolulu/Hawaii/Pacific Ocean
7. Mississippi River
8. Paris/France
9. Denver/Rocky Mountains
10. Mount Fuji/Honshu Island/Japan

To Double or Not to Double` 35

1. darkness 2. dangerous
3. bigger 4. largest
5. cooked 6. flowery
7. avoidance 8. paintable
9. writing 10. creativity
11. cheerful 12. quickly

Tic, Tac, Double 36

1. X X O
O O X
O X O

2. X X O
O O O
O O X

3. X O O
X O X
X X O

4. X O O
O X X
X O X

5. O X X
O X O
X X O

Change the Y to I.............. 37

1. bumpier/bumpiest
2. busier/busiest
3. dustier/dustiest
4. earlier/earliest
5. grayer/grayest
6. prettier/prettiest
7. silliness
8. emptiness
9. happiness
10. sleepiness/sleepily
11. playing
12. studying

Answer Key

Simply Marvelous! 39

1. dangerous
2. breathless
3. treatable
4. hopeful or hopeless
5. wonderful
6. friendly or friendless
7. careful or careless
8. bravely

Dive In 40

1. happy/ness
2. use/ful
3. thin/est
4. spell/ing
5. brave/ly
6. silly/er
7. friend/ly
8. empty/ness
9. smile/ing
10. have/ing
11. comfort/able
12. jog/ed
13. swim/ing
14. peace/ful

Before or After? 41

Color numbers 1, 4, 6, 7, 10, 11, 12, and 14 blue.

Circle the Words 42

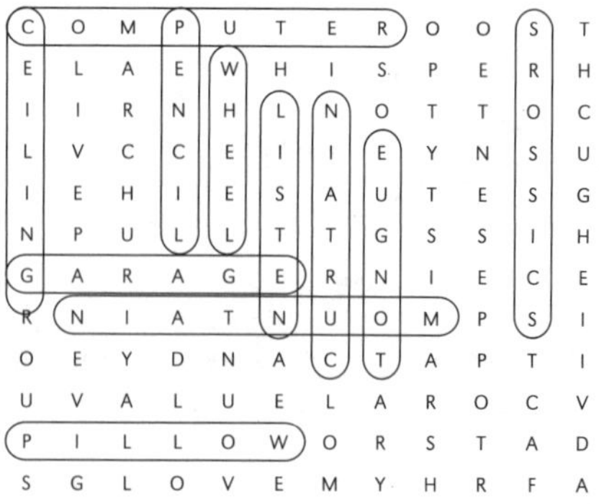

Score a Goal 43

1. ceiling
2. Pillow
3. Wheel
4. garage
5. curtain
6. computer
7. Mountain
8. Tongue
9. Scissors
10. listen

11.–12. Answers will vary.

Test Time (1) 44

1.	neighbor	2.	thought
3.	thumb	4.	ghost
5.	calf	6.	doubt
7.	coaches	8.	waxes
9.	branches	10.	cloud
11.	blouse	12.	scout
13.	flower	14.	porches
15.	butterflies	16.	monkeys
17.	activities	18.	valleys
19.	pennies	20.	puppies
21.	wives	22.	leaves

Test Time (2)........................ 45

Answers will vary.